NOTHING GIVES MORE MONEY THAN THIS

BY

BISHOP OCHEI INNOCENT

COPYRIGHTS RESERVED. NO PART OF THIS PUBLICATION MAY BE REPRODUCED WITHOUT THE WRITTEN PERMISSION OF THE AUTHOR.

Contents

DEDICATION 3

WHY THIS BOOK? 4

Chapter One...10

LISTEN TO THIS STORY 10

Chapter Two 14

THIS IS WHAT HAPPENED TO A HAWKER BY THE ROAD SIDE 14

Chapter Three 17

FROM NOTHING TO SOMETHING ...17

Chapter four 20

BELIEVE ME: PRAYER IS WHAT MADE THE DIFFERENCE IN THESE THREE STORIES! 20

The Bible also tells us that without faith, it is impossible to please God. 22

Chapter Five 23

SINCERELY, YOU CAN TAKE MY WORD TO THE BANK 23

CONSIDER THIS!................................28

OTHER BOOKS BY THE SAME AUTHOR..32

DEDICATION

To the Holy Spirit our Teacher.

WHY THIS BOOK?

Once upon an African village, there were three hunters.

They received news one fine morning that buyers were at the seashore of the city waiting to buy farm fresh game from the hunters.

The first hunter rushed into the bush and shot three antelopes. It took the whole night and much searching because lions and hunters have depleted the antelope stock of the surrounding forest.

With equally much labor, the hunter carried his catch to the buyers.

But they declined buying. "We have enough antelopes of our own" they told him. "So why should we buy yours?"

The Bible tells me that victory is not always to the swift.

The second hunter went first to the buyers and asked what exactly they wanted. They told him.

He rushed into the bush. He forgot that somebody owns the bush.

He was so eager to get the required game that soon as he was in the bush, he began to shoot in the direction he assumed the animal to be. Unknown to him, lions and other predators had earlier frightened away the game. He was shooting towards the east when all the games were in the West! He shot at every shadow and things he believed were moving. As he shot and shot, one of the lions came from behind, attacked, killed and had him for dinner.

The Bible also says it is neither by might nor by power.

The third hunter went to the owners of the land to ask questions and seek their blessings. They know their land inside out. They also knew the buyers well. They understand the antics of the particular game the buyers wanted. The owners of the land also knew how the game would behave at a time like this and the right place to get them. They had the right answers to every question. The third hunter got his directions and blessings and the rest they say is history. He got what the buyers wanted and without extra labor. In digital language, we will say the third hunter worked smart and not necessarily hard.

The owners of the land in this story are like the makers or manufacturers of any product. The manufacturer knows his product. So why go to someone else when you can go to the maker especially when as the manufacturer, he assures you that he is willing to help you?

Have you ever stood at a busy round about? Have you observed how people run from one end of the city to the other? People here are going there in search of what people there are coming here to look for. Everyone is running helter-skelter in search of the same thing. You will be amazed at the rate at which people hire coaches, consultants, counselors, managers, etc, just to tell them in which direction they should go in search of gold.

Very few remember that gold was created by Somebody.

The story has been told of a man who sold his American field and proceeded to South Africa in search of gold only for the man who bought the abandoned field to discover gold on it the next morning! In my sixty years plus on this earth, I have seen many American and European and recently Chinese economic migrants in Africa as well as many African economic migrants in America, Europe and China! Many Americans in Africa died poor and same thing many Africans in America!

In Third World countries, many are still superstitious. They still go to herbalists, shamans, cults, ritual killers and alchemists in search of the proverbial gold.

Unfortunately and as lawyers would say, you cannot give what you do not have. On which continents are these superstitious charlatans predominant: Africa, Asia and remote islands where they only export violence and poverty from.

Somebody created the earth with all the gold and precious stones in it. That person like every manufacturer has written a manual to guide all who dwell on his estate. Why consult Toyota over a

Ford car? When Ford is willing to give you a free sample of his products if only you ask?

This book aims at redirecting those who have gone astray, even in the search for gold, to the Owner of gold and other precious stones on earth and his manual for getting gold and the other precious stones.

Chapter One

LISTEN TO THIS STORY

In 1992, there was a political impasse. The acclaimed winner of the Nigerian presidential election was not acceptable to the military junta. So they refused to declare him winner.

The man himself did not want to be pocketed. So what did he do? He went with some faithful followers to a corner of the nation's capital and declared himself President-elect!

The military declared him wanted. He was to be arrested dead or alive.

He went into hiding.

But the civil society and human rights organizations decided to stand with him. They queried the right of the military maximum ruler to cancel the elections. The maximum ruler and his co-travelers in turn, queried the right of the civil society to query them.

The thing evolved into massive protests. Bonfires were lit where ever police and soldiers were not to be found. And as the soldiers were putting out one fire, protesters would be putting up another.

In the end, anarchy was loosed upon the society and the center could not hold. Light and water supply were cut off. Power and other essentials of life were also cut off from the people. Markets and schools were all closed down. In fact, there was a lockdown in the entire country with emphasis on Lagos.

After a few days, people lacked food. The strikes and protests came without warning. So a lot of people did not have the chance of stocking-piling food at home before the lockdown.

The result was that people began to suffer from starvation. The worst part was that no movement was allowed. If you come out for any reason, either the military personnel will get and classify you as one of those rioting or looters will make a victim of you.

The food of this particular family of six came to zero barely three days of the lockdown. The mother was the home just gave birth. She obviously needed to eat well. The husband did not know what to do. The wife was suffering and so too the other children.

By the seventh day, there was a knock on the door. They were initially afraid to open the door because only soldiers and marauders moved about those days and both were bad news to law abiding citizens.

But they were sore hungry and near surrender. So the wife urged the man to open the door because those at the point of death had nothing more to fear about. The man agreed.

When they opened the door, it was a man they only knew from a distance but who always passed by their door to work or office in times past.

After the exchange of small talk, the man presented a bag of rice and cooking ingredients to the family. He did not forget kerosene for their stove. To the family, manner fell from heaven!

What really happen?

I will tell you after the next story.

Chapter Two

THIS IS WHAT HAPPENED TO A HAWKER BY THE ROAD SIDE

She had tried everything she could but nothing was putting food on her table. All her efforts came to naught.

One day, she met another woman who took pity on her and gave her some part of her own trade wares to sell.

The receive reluctantly accepted them and sat by the roadside sadly watching over her goods but secretly composing what she would say to the good Samaritan that empowered her with the things to sell. She was convinced that the best thing to say to the woman at end of the day was: "did I not tell you?"

But she did not get the chance.

Towards the evening of her first day out with the goods of the other woman, a buyer came, paid for everything the sister had on display and asked for more!

To cut a long story short, after a few supplies to the new buyer, the hawker got a huge order that changed her status for life! She made so much profit that when she walked into the bank; the manager took note of her!

What made the difference in the life of this person who almost committed suicide out of frustration?

Forgive me. I know I promised to tell you what made the difference after the story above but give me a few minutes to tell you of something that happened to me in person. Please bear with me.

Chapter Three

FROM NOTHING TO SOMETHING

Some years back, I had nothing. I could not feed my family. We lived from hand to mouth. Things were so hard that we looked out for castaways and leftovers – crumbs from other people's tables.

I tried my hands at almost everything except the illegal but nothing seemed to be working. I was working like an elephant and yet eating like an ant. I was eating whatever came my way and not what I wanted. My children were constantly sent out of school and I was constantly hiding from the landlord because I could never pay the rent as at when due.

Then one day, a man came into the room where I was and told me a few truths: one of which I am about to share with you now in this book.

He told me what to do to change my story. It was a very simple thing and I did it immediately and my life changed.

Because what he asked me to do was not a ritual or sacrifice requiring much rigor and sacrifice, I almost did not follow the instruction. It took much effort and I dare confess, the Grace of God, for me to obey. I was smitten with the spirit of Neman the leper as told in the famous Bible story. I was pissed off because I had thought that whatever would bring solution into my life would be something hard, loud and long but it was not.

Let me tell you straight away in the next chapter without further ado.

"Those that put their trust in the Lord, shall never see shame"

Chapter four

BELIEVE ME: PRAYER IS WHAT MADE THE DIFFERENCE IN THESE THREE STORIES!

In the first story the family initially succumbed to worry and later to fear. When you find yourself in such situation, devil will begin to magnify the problem and to make them loom larger than life. He knows how to play on our fears and doubts and to make a mountain out of a molehill.

But the family in question was not ignorant of the devices of the devil. They knew that yes, there was a need but that God would never allow a problem bigger than their God to befall them. **They knew that devil is no one else but the father of all liars whose only ministry is to steal, kill and destroy.**

The family knew that the devil easily gets us when we worry. This is a form of disrespect or distrust in God and His abilities. Most times, we act as if we do not know God or His promises or that with God there are impossibilities.

Unlike this family, many persons easily fall to the devil's antics due to ignorance. The bible says in Hosea 4:6 that:

"My people perish for lack of knowledge."

The Bible also tells us that without faith, it is impossible to please God.

Chapter Five

SINCERELY, YOU CAN TAKE MY WORD TO THE BANK

Even if the challenges facing us are as long as windy roads or taller than Atlas mountain, all we need to do is kneel and pray! Go inside the house, close the door, bend your knees and pray! Yes, you heard right: bow before the Lord and ask God for solution!

This simple thing is surprisingly difficult for many because of pride and prejudice. We have preconceived ideas of how treatment is to be carried out on us. So anything short of our expectation must be both false and fake!

Some of us have so programmed ourselves that if we are told crude oil can be had from shale sand, and not deep down the earth or many kilometers down into the belly of the seabed, we say: "impossible". We grew up with a lot of oil rigs running deep down the seas in search of oil that we cannot imagine or accept that that same oil for which we have been prospecting sea beds in vain can be had on the surface! We believe we must dig deep, sweat it out and lose a limb in the process before it makes sense to us. It is nothing but pride

That is why God lamented in **2 Chronicles 7:14** that:

"If my **, who are *called* by *my name*, *will humble themselves* and *pray* and ... then I *will hear* from *heaven*, and I *will* forgive**

their sin and *will heal their land.* ..."

You can see that the problem is a lack of humility. When we find it easy to worry or resort to self help instead of praying, we are exhibiting or being moved by nothing but pride and prejudice.

These, unfortunately, only serve to hinder us. Look at the verse closely. You can see that it is both a call to prayer and a lamentation that if we had long prayed instead of complaining, we would have had solution.

What is it you are looking for that God cannot give?

In **Mathew 7:7** he says:

"Ask and it will be given to you; seek and you will find; knock and the door will be opened to you"

Note that the promise above is a blank check. The Bible did not say what you can ask for and **what you may not ask, including money**! It just says ask and you shall receive.

This is further reinforced in Luke

"Until now you have not asked for anything in my name. Ask and you will receive, and your joy will be complete"

John 16:24

To remove all doubts, here is this scripture:

"Whatever you ask in my name, this will I do that the Father may be glorified in the Son"

John 14: 13

Emphasis here is on the word: **"Whatever". There is neither specification nor limitation to** what you can ask. What so ever you humble yourself and ask, God will give you. Of course, the list includes but not limited to money.

Therefore, open your mouth wide {Psalm 81:10} and ask the Lord of gold and silver if that is where the shoe pinches you and the way he raised the dead, is the same way he blesses with gold and silver!

Chapter Six

CONSIDER THIS!

Many people ask: does God give gold and silver?

The answer is yes. ***Though this should not be our primary motive for coming to Him,*** the point is that if silver and gold are things the devil is using to keep you captive, God will gladly give it to you. God has done it before. He will do it again. He changes not. He makes rich when he is pleased with you and adds no sorrow!

Look at what the scriptures say:

Proverbs 10:22—

"The blessing of the Lord brings wealth, without painful toil for it."

Another one says:

"Moreover, when God gives someone wealth and possessions, and the ability to enjoy them, to accept their lot and be happy in their toil—this is a gift of God.

Ecclesiastes 5:19

Yet, another scripture says God himself gives us the power to create wealth:

Psalms 145:16—

"Thou openest thine hand, and satisfiest the desire of every living thing."

Again, another says:

Philippians 4:19—

"And my God will supply every need of yours according to his riches in glory in Christ Jesus."

Another says:

Job 22:21—

"Submit to God and be at peace with him; in this way, prosperity will come to you."

I can go on and on but to avoid sounding like a broken record, let me stop here with my examples.

Consider that God blessed Abraham.

He blessed Job with gold and silver.

He blessed King David beyond measure.

He blessed Obededom.

He blessed King Solomon with abundant gold and silver.

He blessed Isaac.

He blessed Joseph of Arimathea.

He can and will bless you too if you ask.

ABOUT THE AUTHOR

Bishop Ochei Innocent, 62, has been a born-again Christian for over thirty years.

He holds degrees in Theology and Ministry.

He trained and worked secularly as a journalist and rose to be an editor before retiring into the church.

He is currently the President of New Dimension Seminaries International with presence in several countries., training and strengthening thousands of clergy men and women.

He is married with four children: spirit-filled two boys and two girls. Above all, he is a called teacher who enjoys writing more than eating food.

OTHER BOOKS BY THE SAME AUTHOR

1. SEVEN BIBILICAL QUESTIONS MOST CHRISTIANS CANNOT ANSWER.
2. FORTY MAJOR EVANGELISM MISTAKES MOST CHURCHES MAKE
3. HOW TO KNOW A MAD PASTOR
4. SOMETHING WORSE THAN WITCHCRAFT
5. SO YOU CALL YOURSELF A MANAGER?
6. CONTEMPORARY CHRISTIAN MINISTRY: VOL.1-5
7. FORTY ABOMINABLE WORDS THAT SHOULD NEVE R COME OUT OF THE MOUTH OF A PENTECOSTAL PASTOR

8. HOW A CHRISTIAN CAN RECEIVE CASH DAILY
9. EIGHT SIMPLE WAYS TO ATTEND A SEMINAR WITHOUT PAYING.
10. WHY A CHRISTIAN SHOULD NOT BE CALLED AUGUSTINE
11. OVERCOMING THE POWER OF WITCHCRAFT
12. SIXTY THINGS YOU MUST DO BEFORE AGE SIXTY
13. TEN THINGS I LIKE ABOUT THE BIBLE
14. TEN THINGS I LIKE ABOUT AFRICA'S RICHEST MAN
15. APOSTASY: HOW ONE CAN FALL INTO IT WITHOUT KNOWING.
16. DANGERS OF ORDINATION AND WHY WHO ORDAINS YOU MATTERS.
17. THE BANISHED PASTOR

18. TWENTY THINGS A LOUSY WOMAN WILL NEVER TELL HER DAUGHTER
19. PASTORS WORKBOOK FOR MINISTRY AND SELF BRANDING
20. WHY I PAY THITHE
21. HOW SHE DESTROYED HER HOME
22. WHAT HAPPENS WHEN AN AMERICAN PREACHER VISITS AFRICA?
23. I WISH SOMEBODY TOLD ME THIS BEFORE
24. WHAT HAPPENS WHEN AN AMERICAN PREACHER COMES TO AFRICA
25. HOW TO CONNECT AND KEEP YOUR MINISTERIAL CONTACTS
26. ETC

NOTES

NOTES

NOTES

NOTES

www.ingramcontent.com/pod-product-compliance
Lightning Source LLC
Chambersburg PA
CBHW030738180526
45157CB00008BA/3222